# DREAMERS HAVE A DREAM TOO

ED ESCOTO

ISBN: 197767223X
ISBN-13: 978-1977672230

## DEDICATION

This book is dedicated to all the Dreamers who are fighting for their chance at the American Dream. Rest easier knowing there are many who have empathy for your struggle and will stand in solidarity with you. We are all people first. We are all dreamers.

> "Our lives begin to end the day we become silent about things that matter."

Martin Luther King Jr.

# CONTENTS

PART 1 – I HAVE A DREAM

PART 2 – THE DREAMER'S DREAM

PART 3 – WE ARE ALL DREAMERS

ADDITIONAL RESOURCES

THANK YOU

ABOUT THE AUTHOR

ALSO BY THE AUTHOR

CHILDREN'S BOOKS

*Amazon #1 Best Seller, Derek and Haylee Learn Spanish*

*Amazon #1 Best Seller, My First Spanish Words*

*My First Alphabet Book*

*Life of a Stick Kid*

OTHER BOOKS

*Divorced Before 30*

# 1

## I HAVE A DREAM

WHEN WE LOOK BACK throughout history, there are movements that altered the course of human history and this nation for generations to come. Truly pivotal moments that propelled us forward and redefined what it means to be a person and an American. Many great movements can trace their genesis to a single individual – a moment – a dream.

What is arguably the most significant speech given in the past century, Martin Luther King Jr.'s *I Have a Dream* speech that rippled through the Lincoln Memorial and beyond on that summer day will forever be a reminder of how powerful a dream can be.

When we forget our past, we are destined to repeat it. His words inspired a nation in 1963 and their significance is not absent today.

Trying to interpret Dr. King's heart-gripping words on that hot August day can never do them justice, so I felt you should experience his hope-filled words for yourself.

∞

**I Have a Dream** – August 28, 1963

"I am happy to join with you today in what will go down in history as the greatest demonstration for freedom in the history of our nation.

Five score years ago, a great American, in whose symbolic shadow we stand today, signed the Emancipation Proclamation. This momentous decree came as a great beacon light of hope to millions of Negro slaves who had been seared in the flames of withering injustice. It came as a joyous daybreak to end the long night of their captivity.

But one hundred years later, the Negro still is not free. One hundred years later, the life of the Negro is still sadly crippled by the manacles of segregation and the chains of discrimination. One hundred years later, the Negro lives on a lonely island of poverty in the midst of a vast ocean of material prosperity. One hundred years later, the Negro is still languishing in the corners of American society and finds himself an exile in his own land. So we have come here today to dramatize a shameful condition.

In a sense, we have come to our nation's capital to cash a check. When the architects of our republic wrote the magnificent words of the Constitution and the Declaration of Independence, they were signing a promissory note to which every American was to fall heir. This note was a promise that all men, yes, black men as well as white men, would be guaranteed the unalienable rights of life, liberty, and the pursuit of happiness.

It is obvious today that America has defaulted on this promissory note insofar as her citizens of color are concerned. Instead of honoring this sacred obligation, America has given the Negro people a bad check, a check which has come back marked "insufficient funds." But we refuse to believe that the bank of justice is bankrupt. We refuse to believe that there are insufficient funds in the great vaults of opportunity of this nation. So we have come to cash this check — a check that will give us upon demand the riches of freedom and the security of justice.

We have also come to this hallowed spot to remind America of the fierce urgency of now. This is no time to engage in the luxury of cooling off or to take the tranquilizing drug of gradualism. Now is the time to make real the promises of democracy. Now is the time to rise from the dark and desolate valley of segregation to the sunlit path of racial justice. Now is the time to lift our nation from the quick sands of racial injustice to the solid rock of brotherhood. Now is the time to make justice a reality for all of God's children. .

It would be fatal for the nation to overlook the urgency of the moment. This sweltering summer of the Negro's legitimate discontent will not pass until there is an invigorating autumn of freedom and equality. Nineteen sixty-three is not an end, but a beginning. Those who hope that the Negro needed to blow off steam and will now be content will have a rude awakening if the nation returns to business as usual. There will be neither rest nor tranquility in America until the Negro is granted his citizenship rights. The whirlwinds of revolt will continue to shake the foundations of our nation until the bright day of justice emerges.

But there is something that I must say to my people who stand on the warm threshold which leads into the palace of justice. In the process of gaining our rightful place we must not be guilty of wrongful deeds. Let us not seek to satisfy our thirst for freedom by drinking from the cup of bitterness and hatred.

We must forever conduct our struggle on the high plane of dignity and discipline. We must not allow our creative protest to degenerate into physical violence. Again and again we must rise to the majestic heights of meeting physical force with soul force. The marvelous new militancy which has engulfed the Negro community must not lead us to a distrust of all white people, for many of our white brothers, as evidenced by their presence here today, have come to realize that their destiny is tied up with our destiny. They have come to realize that their freedom is inextricably bound to our freedom. We cannot walk alone.

As we walk, we must make the pledge that we shall always march ahead. We cannot turn back. There are those who are asking the devotees of civil rights, "When will you be satisfied?" We can never be satisfied as long as the Negro is the victim of the unspeakable horrors of police brutality. We can never be satisfied, as long as our bodies, heavy with the fatigue of travel, cannot gain lodging in the motels of the highways and the hotels of the cities.

We cannot be satisfied as long as the Negro's basic mobility is from a smaller ghetto to a larger one. We can never be satisfied as long as our children are stripped of their selfhood and robbed of their dignity by signs stating "For Whites Only". We cannot be satisfied as long as a Negro in Mississippi cannot vote and a Negro in New York believes he has nothing for which to vote. No, no, we are not satisfied, and we will not be satisfied until justice rolls down like waters and righteousness like a mighty stream.

I am not unmindful that some of you have come here out of great trials and tribulations. Some of you have come fresh from narrow jail cells. Some of you have come from areas where your quest for freedom left you battered by the storms of persecution and staggered by the winds of police brutality. You have been the veterans of creative suffering. Continue to work with the faith that unearned suffering is redemptive.

Go back to Mississippi, go back to Alabama, go back to South Carolina, go back to Georgia, go back to Louisiana, go back to the slums and ghettos of our northern cities, knowing that somehow this situation can and will be changed. Let us not wallow in the valley of despair.

I say to you today, my friends, so even though we face the difficulties of today and tomorrow, I still have a dream. It is a dream deeply rooted in the American dream.

I have a dream that one day this nation will rise up and live out the true meaning of its creed: "We hold these truths to be self-evident: that all men are created equal."

I have a dream that one day on the red hills of Georgia the sons of former slaves and the sons of former slave owners will be able to sit down together at the table of brotherhood.

I have a dream that one day even the state of Mississippi, a state sweltering with the heat of injustice, sweltering with the heat of oppression, will be transformed into an oasis of freedom and justice.

I have a dream that my four little children will one day live in a nation where they will not be judged by the color of their skin but by the content of their character. I have a dream today.

I have a dream that one day, down in Alabama, with its vicious racists, with its governor having his lips dripping with the words of interposition and nullification; one day right there in Alabama, little black boys and black girls will be able to join hands with little white boys and white girls as sisters and brothers. I have a dream today.

I have a dream that one day every valley shall be exalted, every hill and mountain shall be made low, the rough places will be made plain, and the crooked places will be made straight, and the glory of the Lord shall be revealed, and all flesh shall see it together.

This is our hope. This is the faith that I go back to the South with. With this faith we will be able to hew out of the mountain of despair a stone of hope. With this faith we will be able to transform the jangling discords of our nation into a beautiful symphony of brotherhood. With this faith we will be able to work together, to pray together, to struggle together, to go to jail together, to stand up for freedom together, knowing that we will be free one day.

This will be the day when all of God's children will be able to sing with a new meaning, "My country, 'tis of thee, sweet land of liberty, of thee I sing. Land where my fathers died, land of the pilgrim's pride, from every mountainside, let freedom ring."

And if America is to be a great nation this must become true. So let freedom ring from the prodigious hilltops of New Hampshire. Let freedom ring from the mighty mountains of New York. Let freedom ring from the heightening Alleghenies of Pennsylvania. Let freedom ring from the snowcapped Rockies of Colorado. Let freedom ring from the curvaceous slopes of California.

But not only that; let freedom ring from Stone Mountain of Georgia. Let freedom ring from Lookout Mountain of Tennessee. Let freedom ring from every hill and molehill of Mississippi. From every mountainside, let freedom ring.

And when this happens, when we allow freedom to ring, when we let it ring from every village and every hamlet, from every state and every city, we will be able to speed up that day when all of God's children, black men and white men, Jews and Gentiles, Protestants and Catholics, will be able to join hands and sing in the words of the old Negro spiritual, Free at last, free at last. Great God Almighty, we are free at last."

# 2

## THE DREAMER'S DREAM

FOLLOWING IN THE FOOTSTEPS of the great Civil Rights' leader and the movement which has made progress in the decades following Dr. King's unforgettable speech, more work remains to be done. Our country and its people are not perfect; nor shall we ever be, but the flame of fortitude will not fade. Martin Luther King Jr.'s Dream remains in the hearts and minds of many.

The nearly 800,000 Dreamers who came out from living in the shadows five years ago also have a dream. This dream doesn't stem from outright racial injustice, although the embers of hate can never fully extinguished as long as people walk on God's green Earth.

The Dreamer's dream is akin to the great dreams that came before: It is deeply rooted in the American Dream.

This dream is the result of arriving to the United States as children through no fault of their own. An unintended consequence of good people who simply wanted a better life for their family, so they packed what they could, and brought their children to America.

The Dreamer's dream is one of humility and humanity: An opportunity to go after the American Dream. Nothing more. Not a handout or welfare. Simply an opportunity to provide for themselves and their family without the crippling fear of deportation.

It's truly astounding as to how many people are in favor of supporting Dreamers and DACA, yet this topic remains such a hot-button issue in political circles.

The Declaration of Independence states, "We hold these truths to be self-evident, that all men are created equal, that they are endowed by their Creator with certain unalienable Rights, that among these are Life, Liberty and the pursuit of Happiness."

I firmly believe the majority of people who oppose Dreamers do not have hate in their hearts. It is difficult to empathize with the struggles of others if you haven't been in a similar position yourself. For someone born in this great country, they don't understand what it truly means to "get in line and do it the right way."

If you're a teenage boy in a crime-ravaged country such as El Salvador, "get in line" means you will either join a gang or be forced to join. "Get in line" for that boy means a forced life of crime or starve. For that boy, this mythical line to perceived-prosperity leads straight to prison or an early grave.

There are others who could emphasize, but choose not to for various reasons. One reason stems from a fear of the unknown. For example, to a woman born and raised in a small town in the Midwest where the majority of people look and talk the same, the thought of people coming from far-away countries who don't fit the normal Midwest mold, could worry her.

It wouldn't be the first time this country had fear or even a distaste for immigrants.

Refugees seeking haven in America were poor and disease-ridden. They threatened to take jobs away from Americans and use valuable welfare dollars. They worshiped a different religion and pledged allegiance to a foreign leader. They were accused of being rapists. These undesirables were Irish.

Although most certainly tired and poor, the Irish did not arrive in America yearning to breathe free; they simply wanted to eat. Native-born citizens and former immigrants alike felt threatened. Help wanted signs would even read "Irish Need Not Apply."

Unfortunately, there are people who have hate in their hearts and their current targets are immigrants and Dreamers. Whether it's their upbringing or a developed taste for hate, they do exist. The trigger that awakens the hate within these people can be the Dreamer's place of birth, color of their skin, or a myriad of other reasons. We can't do anything for these revolting excuse for human beings. Our only solace comes from the hope that this hateful mindset doesn't infect the minds of little ones.

I truly believe most people are kind and have good intentions. I also believe those who oppose Dreamers, do so out of convenience, a false-narrative that is perpetuated, or simply haven't been exposed to new information. After all, we generally tend to surround ourselves with people who think, believe, and behave in similar ways. It's human nature.

Immigration is a complicated topic that is made up of many layers, but when it comes to Dreamers, things become more simple and the numbers speak for themselves.

∞

**HERE'S SOME STATS YOU SHOULD KNOW**

1. There are more than 43 million immigrants in the United States, according to the Migration Policy Institute.

2. About 11 million are undocumented immigrants.

3. An estimated 22 percent of undocumented immigrants are under age 25, according to the Department of Homeland Security.

4. The Migration Policy Institute said in 2016 that about 1.9 million people were eligible for DACA.

5. About 788,000 have had their requests for DACA status accepted, according to U.S. Citizenship and Immigration Services.

6. In order to apply for DACA, immigrants had to be younger than 31 on June 15, 2012.

7. DACA applicants must have come to the U.S. before turning 16. They must have lived in the U.S. since June 15, 2007.

8. In a Center for American Progress survey of roughly 3,000 DACA recipients, nine-tenths of respondents had jobs.

9. About 72 percent of respondents were in higher education.

10. Their average hourly wage was $17.46 an hour, up from $10.29 before receiving DACA.

11. After getting DACA, nearly 80 percent of respondents said they gained driver's licenses. About half became organ donors.

12. A Morning Consult poll from found that 56 percent of registered voters said Dreamers, another name for people who came to the U.S. as kids, "should be allowed to stay and become citizens if they meet certain requirements."

13. The Center for American Progress estimated that the U.S. would lose about $460 billion in GDP over the next 10 years without DACA.

14. About 700,000 people could lose their jobs.

15. More than 1,800 governors, attorneys general, mayors, state representatives, judges, police chiefs and other leaders signed onto a letter supporting Dreamers and DACA recipients.

∞

The various ways in which Dreamers contribute to our nation can never be fully quantified. There is an uncalculatable amount of value that a human being can add to society apart from what they receive in benefits versus the amount they contribute in taxes. Think about it. Most of us attended public schools as kids which was a huge investment by taxpayers because we have decided as a society that some things are simply "worth it."

How do you put a value on the benefits of culture, diversity, kindness, serving in the U.S. Armed Forces, and being a good neighbor and person?

There are many ways in which Dreamers contribute to this nation, many of which can't be quantified. But some can.

∞

1. **Dreamers dramatically increase the pool of highly qualified recruits for the U.S. Armed Forces.**

David S. C. Chu, Bush Administration Under Secretary, Personnel and Readiness, Department of Defense said, "many of these young people may wish to join the military, and have the attributes needed – education, aptitude, fitness, and moral qualifications. In fact, many are High School Diploma Graduates, and may have fluent language skills — both in English and their native language. Provisions of S. 2611, such as the DREAM Act, would provide these young people the opportunity of serving the United States in uniform."

There is a strong tradition of military service in immigrant families, but the lack of immigration status prevents many who wish to serve from enlisting. According to Margaret Stock, Lieutenant Colonel (ret.), Military Police Corps, US Army Reserve and Associate

Professor of Law, United States Military Academy, West Point, NY – The DREAM Act "would allow military recruiters to enlist this highly qualified cohort of young people, and enactment of the DREAM Act would be a 'win-win' scenario for the Department of Defense and the United States. Deporting these young people … deprives the United States of a valuable human asset that can be put to work in the Global War on Terrorism."

2. **Dreamers are supported by 70 percent of likely voters and by leaders in education, the military, business and religious orders.**

A national poll of 1,008 adults, conducted by Opinion Research Corporation for First Focus, shows that support cuts across regional and party lines with 70 percent overall support, 60% support from Republicans and 80% support from Democrats.

3. **Supporting Dreamers is a great return on money we have already invested and will prepare the country for the global economy.**

The students who benefit under the DREAM Act have been raised and educated in the U.S. State and local taxpayers have already invested in the education of these children in elementary and secondary school. America deserves a return on their investment.

Today's global economy requires an educated and skilled workforce capable of acquiring, creating, and distributing knowledge.

The Bureau of Labor Statistics (BLS) "estimates that many of the occupations that will be most in demand in years to come will rely on highly educated workers. Of the 15 occupations projected to grow at least twice as fast as the national average (13 percent), 10 require an associate degree or higher." For this reason "it is imperative to develop policies …to help these talented students gain access to postsecondary educational opportunities and the workforce as legal residents."

Leading businesses such as Microsoft have endorsed the DREAM Act because they recognize that our broken immigration system is draining our economy of the talent and resources needed to compete in the global economy.

## 4. Dreamers help reduce high school dropout rates and enable more students to attend college.

Foreign-born students represent a significant and growing percentage of the current student population. Unfortunately, immigration status and the associated barriers to higher education contribute to a higher-than-average high school dropout rate, which costs taxpayers and the economy billions of dollars each year. The

DREAM Act eliminates these barriers for many students, and the DREAM Act's high school graduation requirement would provide a powerful incentive for students who might otherwise drop out to stay in school and graduate.

## 5. Dreamers increase revenues in our communities.

Enabling 800,000 immigrant students access to higher education would go a long way in inspiring other immigrant youth to strive for a college education. This will help boost the number of high skilled American-raised workers. As they take their place in the workplace as hard working, taxpaying Americans, they will contribute a lifetime of revenues at the local, state and federal level.

## 6. The Economics of Dreamers.

"Dreamers contribute to the labor supply, a particularly important dimension of the economic argument, as our aging workforce is responsible for 70 percent of the predicted slowdown in potential economic growth, according to the Congressional Budget Office. Dreamers contribute more than they receive in benefits from the tax and Social Security systems.

The cost of providing public education, for example, are clear, but the benefits are difficult to measure and appear in ways that advanced societies have long agreed are worth it. We have no surveys that talk to patients about the quality of the help they get from immigrant health care professionals, and how much that improves their well-being. We don't include the inherent cultural benefits of diversity in our schools, as our children learn essential lessons that may, if we're lucky, lead future generations to live with each other a lot more peacefully than we do today.

Even the standard economic analysis is flawed. Undocumented workers are already here, and if they're working, they're doing so in the shadows, often with none of the standard labor protections. That puts both native-born workers and immigrants at a disadvantage as well, incentivizing employers to race to the bottom. In fact, there's research showing that implementing DACA status on undocumented workers raises not just their pay, but also the pay of those they work with.

The "taking-our-jobs" analysis is equally flawed. The idea that there's a fixed number of jobs to go around and, if you've got one, that's one less for me isn't true. But anyone who's here, whether an immigrant or a nonimmigrant, doesn't just create labor supply. They create labor demand. They consume housing, food, transportation, and so on. Instead of replacing other workers, their work often complements the jobs of other workers allowing, for example, other workers to move up the occupation ladder.

At the end of the day, it is impossible to determine a person's total economic value. All we can know is - does someone want to be here among us and do they agree to play by the rules. Dreamers pass both these tests with flying colors."

∞

Let's take a step back. It can be easy to get lost in the details and lose sight of the bigger picture. Ignore all the numbers for a moment. Forget about all the arguments that oppose or support Dreamers. As is true with most things in life, when you peel back all the layers, things become pretty simple.

Can you look yourself in the mirror and say that a Dreamer who was brought to this country at the age of 10 should be punished for the actions of his parents? What if he was three months old? Should a three month old be punished because his parents took him with them while they stole a car?

That three month old baby may now be 25 years old, is it right to punish him for something he had no control over that many years ago?

∞

When we categorize and label an entire group of people, we unknowingly diminish their humanity. That leads to a lack of empathy which in turn allows once decent human beings to treat others less than human.

Slavery was the result of a large segment of society believing that African Americans were less than human. In fact, at one point in time, they were considered 1/8 of a man. There are countless moments in our nation and world's history that makes me lower my head in disgust and say, "How could we fucking ignore so much injustice?"

Fortunately, we now live in a nation that has progressed enough that most people believe slavery, lynching homosexuals, disrespecting women and minorities is wrong and should not be tolerated.

∞

For the 800,000 Dreamers, the individual gets lost in the label. Although they are supported by many, Dreamers face vocal opposition and are labeled as "illegals." They endure the unrelenting onslaught of "go back to where you came from' and "we don't want you here."

It's important that our humanity as a nation not sway. If we allow injustice anywhere, we allow injustice everywhere. We're not talking about 800,000 Dreamers, we're talking about one Rodrigo, one Julia, one Hiram, one Ari, one Denis.

# Rodrigo's Story

"My name is Rodrigo, and I'm 20 years old. I'm from Mexico, a place I have little recollection about since my departure from Mexico to the U.S when I was six years old. Adapting wasn't so difficult, I picked up the English language at a fast pace, due to my eagerness to learn new things. I would get picked on once in a while because of my broken English, but that only motivated me.

When I was in the 11th grade my step dad was deported, but he had a conversation with me before he was sent back to Mexico. He told me that I was going to have to be the man of the house because he didn't think he was ever coming back. I didn't know what he was trying to say at the time, until he passed away crossing the U.S border. He couldn't bear to be away from his family.

When I received the news that my step dad passed away, I fell into depression because I had lost my father figure. At the same time, I felt uncertain about continuing high school, because I did not know undocumented students could go to college. These two events led me to drop out of school.

When I was out of school I tried to get a job but because of my undocumented status, most places rejected me. I soon realized I made a huge mistake by dropping out, so at the age of 19, I decided to go back to school and I graduated in 2014 at the age of 20.

I heard about Deferred Action for Childhood Arrivals, DACA, from family members and I applied because of the opportunity that it brings to those of us who want to continue our education. I am motivated by knowing that I can get a job after earning a degree, which would be a big achievement. After attending the DACA clinics I am no longer scared to say I'm undocumented. I plan to continue my studies and want to help others who have the potential of becoming someone great but because of similar life circumstances, don't believe in themselves. In the next three years I see myself working, and graduating college with a bachelor's degree in business."

## Julia's Story

"When I was 9, my family and I moved to United States to find some stability that wasn't present in our home country. We always had plans to make the move permanent, and the seemingly endless paperwork process began nearly immediately.

However, we didn't know what we were in for. The lawyer we had turned out to be fraudulent, and as a result, my parents, my sisters and I all lost our status in the country. It was the summer before my first year of high school.

The future remained unclear, but I made some choices. I chose to keep my grades up in school. I chose to give myself the opportunity at a future. I worked hard. I graduated 28th in a class of 620. I had a 3.6. I got into Rutgers early admission.

The week after my twenty-first birthday, I got notice that my DACA application had been approved. Within 12 hours, I'd applied for a social security card, and within a week, I'd filled out dozens of job applications. I got a license, for the first time, ever.

In November 2014, I got into Teach For America. I was placed in San Antonio, 1,800 miles away from New Jersey. I graduated college the following May, cum laude, with a double-major in English and Journalism.

In August 2015, I started teaching. I also met the man that would become the love of my life. I had a new life in a new state and I was all by myself for the first time ever, and I couldn't be more excited.

I've been teaching middle school since then, and I love it. My kids are amazing. They drive me nuts on any given day, but I love them.

DACA gave me my independence back. It's the single reason I am able to teach, and live on my own, and pay for my car, and feel like I belong in the country I have lived in for 15 years.

Knowing that I could lose all the freedom I've gained is a paralyzing fear. I've worked so hard, and my life was just coming together, and now it might fall apart again. I hope that doesn't happen, but if I've learned anything these last 15 years, it's to hope for the best and prepare for the worst."

# Hiram's Story

"Fear, stress, anxiety, hunger, anger, pain... these are all symptoms the typical American doesn't feel on a daily basis but unfortunately for many of us it is our everyday reality. Maybe not all symptoms at once, but at one point or another we feel them.

I was brought to this country just before my fourth birthday and have been here ever since. Now at 28, I have attended and graduated from one of the best public schools in the nation, help my younger (US born) brother pay for that same university, have encouraged my younger (US born) sister to attend and have inspired an entire generation of younger cousins to look forward to college.

With the help of DACA, I have been able to do things and contribute to society in a way I could never have imagined. I spend most of my days focusing on my career as a licensed architect, but I also dedicate a large portion of my time to mentoring and educating the less fortunate population on the importance of education and moving forward. I'm not an activist, but I feel passionately about real world situations that affect not only me, but those around me and society as we know it. The rhetoric currently being spread is toxic to the growing generation and I believe it is crucial for true and rational statements to be made by those in power.

Whatever happens after January 20th is out of my power but I truly hope my current contributions, and those of thousands of others, will not be ignored. We are as American as the person standing next to us at Subway other Jimmy John's … 9 digits should not define our ability to contribute to society and neither should a document saying we are temporarily able to… I'm not asking for the entire pie, I'm simply asking for acknowledgement and acceptance."

## Ari's Story

"I was brought to the US when I was 12 years old. My parents tried adjusting status but were misguided by an immigration attorney. My birth country was in a severe recession at the time and we could not go back as we did not have any means to survive back there so we stayed. I was always kind of aware of our immigration status, but it wasn't until it came time to applying to colleges that I really began to understand what it meant to be an undocumented immigrant. I graduated with high honors, however I knew I could not go to a 4 year college as I had no means of paying for it. I ended up going to a community college and earned an associate's degree in 2010 after 5 years as I had to work full-time earning a little more than the minimum wage to pay for the out-of-state tuition.

The 2012 DACA was a blessing, I applied promptly, got the fingerprinting done and got approved within 3 months. After being granted DACA I was able to find a better job and go back to school- I graduated and now hold a bachelor's degree in business administration.

I'm now a proud home owner and have started my own business. The fear of losing everything I have is real, the fear of getting deported to a country I don't know is real. I'm a tax payer, entrepreneur, an Undocumented American. I have lived here for 17 years and this is my home, this is the country I love."

## Denis' Story

"I didn't cry. I knew it was for the best. I said goodbye to many: the people I love. I felt uncertainty. Yet, I didn't cry.

You see, I knew of the American dream. Every evening I'd watch American films filled with white picket fences, and big city aspirations. I dreamed of setting foot in the land of opportunity.

After a dangerous journey we arrived home. Every morning I pledged allegiance to the flag. I meant it. I excelled in school. That why our parents worked so hard; why we risked so much; opportunities that'd come through education and hard work.

Later, I learned what my undocumented status truly meant, I was felt uncertainty, shame: no future. Rattled by depression, I contemplated giving up.

Luckily, I had educators that'd tell me I was wasting a mind. So I've continued to pursue my education and help run our family business.

Through DACA, me and 800,000 others live freely. We can contribute, that's our American dream: that's why my mother works so hard, hands aching, yet a kind smile on her face. That's why I study economics, to one day enthrall my mind to the betterment of this nation.

I watched Trump make his way to the podium, I felt uncertainty. My own need for an answer was channeled, through the screen, into the mind of a reporter who asked about DACA. No answer. Silence.

The 45th President took office. Cannons fired; people applauded; rain fell. But, I do not believe in omens. If the life of 800,000 "DACAmented" Americans is altered it will not be by virtue of the rain. It will be by the lightning strike of one man's hand.

We ask Donald Trump to consider the ramifications of that action. It's estimated that ending DACA will lead to 450 billion dollars lost. Our ask, however is more than an economic matter. It is a matter of principle and morality. We ask for nothing more than what we deserve. The cost, we will continue to pay with the sweat of our brow and the pounding of our passionate hearts - As we've always done, day in and day out.

We ask only to let us contribute freely. Let us walk along you, shoulder to shoulder, on that same road our hands help to pave. Human decency and morality demand it. The American people, our people, demand it."

# 3

## WE ARE ALL DREAMERS

A T THE END OF THE DAY, we are more alike than we are different. We all love this country and want to build a better future here. We are all after the same thing - a chance to go after the American dream.

**WE ARE ALL DREAMERS**

Edgar
Father of two and proud son of two immigrants.
Texas

Stefanie
Proud daughter of an immigrant doctor.
Texas

Juan
Proud immigrant, husband, grandfather of two,
and father of a teacher, attorney, and the Author
of this book.
Texas

Robert
Father of twins, husband, and soldier.
Afghanistan

Karina
University of Phoenix alumni and Human
Resources professional.
California

Stan
Father of two.
California

Erick
Father of 2, husband, and entrepreneur.
Texas

Elizabeth
Mom of 3, wife, and nursing student.
California

Luceyda
Single mother of 3 beautiful daughters and
Mortgage Advisor.
California

Gerardo
Digital Engineer for Canon, son of two
immigrants, husband of an immigrant, and father
of two honor roll students.
Texas

Kayla
Strong hardworking mother, daughter, sister,
and friend.
Florida

Mike
Husband and father.
Arizona

Jesus
Son of immigrant parents and student.
Illinois

Rochelle
Student and server.
New York

Priscilla
Web Consultant and bartender.
Georgia

Beatriz
Insurance Agent.
Texas

Oriana
Mother and brand designer.
California

Ralph
Son, brother, fellow human being.
California

Susie
Mother of 2 and solutions specialist.
Texas

Andrea
Candidate for Master's Degree in Environmental
Engineering.
California

Mason
Husband, father, and EMT.
Nevada

Alexandria
Corporate Marketing
Florida

Sophia
Dog mom, bartender, and yogi.
California

James
Project Manager, runner, and activist.
Oregon

Isabelle
Social media influencer and fitness enthusiast.
Florida

Liam
College football player and son of an immigrant
mother.
Ohio

Mayra
Accountant Office Administrator, wife, soccer
mom, daughter of immigrant parents.
Texas

Ann
Teacher for 15 years and cat mom.
South Carolina

Samantha
Journalist and blogger.
Washington, D.C.

Miguel
Small business owner and barber.
New Mexico

Mary
Mother, wife and proud American.
North Carolina

Olivia
Teacher and proud daughter of an immigrant
father.
Washington

Noah
Producer, director, and activist.
California

Ben
Father and son of a beautiful immigrant mother.
Texas

Sebastian
Husband and firefighter.
Nevada

River
Human and lover of all things of this Earth.
California

Emily
Future mother in two months and social media
manager.
New York

Skylar
Dancer and poet.
California

Anthony
Father of 3 girls and husband.
Virginia

Mark
Uncle and electrician.
Michigan

Emily
Single mother of two girls and sales manager.
Florida

Luna
Executive assistant and aspiring chef.
Arizona

Nathan
Bank teller and student.
Texas.

David
Father of 2, grandfather of 3, and Vietnam
Veteran.
California

Evelyn
Accountant, MBA, and CPA.
California

Matt
Husband and small business owner.
Kentucky

Maya
Student and barista.
California

Sean
Personal trainer and meditation junkie.
California

Martha
Proud mommy of two honor roll students and
Realtor.
California

Jackie
Entrepreneur and getting master's degree.
New York

Jennifer
Aunt to an amazing niece and a nurse for 27
years.
Illinois

Jeff
Retail operations manager and starting a new
business.
Washington

Lucy
In love with a dreamer and business student.
Texas

I have a confession to make. Not everyone on
the list is a Dreamer. Many are people who have
empathy for their struggle and simply want to
stand in solidarity with Dreamers.

**Can you tell who is a Dreamer and who
isn't simply by reading their name?**

I didn't think so.

I am not a Dreamer according to the DREAM Act of DACA since I won the ultimate lottery when I was born in this country, but I do share the Dreamer's dream. There is one thing that unites each name that was read: We are working hard and trying to better ourselves and our communities. We all want a better life for our kids and family.

As we look back throughout history, what is just and right becomes evident. I don't want the next generation to look back and wonder why good people stood silent and did nothing.

---

**"The ultimate measure of a man is not where he stands in moments of comfort and convenience, but where he stands at times of challenge and controversy."**

Martin Luther King Jr.

---

At the end of the day, we are more alike than we are different. We all love this country and want to build a better future here. We are all after the same thing - a chance to go after the American dream.

WE ARE ALL DREAMERS

# ADDITIONAL RESOURCES

If you are interested in finding additional information about this topic or simply want to stay informed, I found some organizations that are a great place to start. These organizations are supporting and standing alongside Dreamers as they navigate through the uncertainty.

In doing research for this book and through conversations with people who are intimately involved with DACA and Dreamers, I strongly feel the following organizations are making a real difference and doing great work.

## Immigrant Legal Resource Center

The mission of the Immigrant Legal Resource Center (ILRC) is to work with and educate immigrants, community organizations, and the legal sector to continue to build a democratic society that values diversity and the rights of all people.

Website: www.ilrc.org

## National Immigration Law Center

Established in 1979, the National Immigration Law Center (NILC) is one of the leading organizations in the U.S. exclusively dedicated to defending and advancing the rights of immigrants with low income.

Website: www.nilc.org

## Educators For Fair Consideration

E4FC's mission is to empower undocumented young people to achieve their academic and career goals and actively contribute to society. Over the past seven years, we have grown to offer an array of programs and services that holistically address the needs of undocumented young people through direct support, leadership development, community outreach, and advocacy.

Website: www.e4fc.org

## Immigrant Defense Project

The Immigrant Defense Project works to secure fairness and justice for immigrants in the United States.

Website: www.immigrantdefenseproject.org

## TheDream.US

The DREAM.US is the nation's largest college access and success program for Dreamers. Working with our partners, we provide scholarships to highly-motivated Dreamers to help them pay for their college education.

Website: www.thedream.us

## Border Angels

Border Angels is an all-volunteer, non-profit organization that advocates for human rights, humane immigration reform, and social justice with a special focus on issues related to issues related to the US-Mexican border.

Website: www.borderangels.org

# THANK YOU

I hope you enjoyed *Dreamers Have a Dream Too!*

I truly enjoyed creating this book and thank you for allowing me to share this with you.

DACA and the DREAM Act has a profound impact on hundreds of thousands of people. I only hope this book helps expand the conversation and maybe even change someone's opinion regarding Dreamers.

As an author, I love feedback. You are the reason I write. Tell me what you liked, what you loved, and even what you hated. I'd love to hear from you. Write me at Ed@EdEscoto.com or 310.774.7992.

Finally, I need to ask a favor. I'd love a review of *Dreamers Have a Dream Too*. Reviews can be tough to come by these days. You, the reader, have the power to make or break a book. If you have the time, visit edescoto.com which has all my books and links to Amazon where you can write a review.

Thank you so much for reading *Dreamers Have a Dream Too*.

With gratitude,
Ed Escoto

# ABOUT THE AUTHOR

Ed Escoto is first and foremost, a dad to two amazing kids. Other than his kids, his passion revolves around creating things and adding life to his years.

He is a writer and self-proclaimed minimalist.

He is the author of six books in multiple genres. Several of his books became Amazon #1 Best-Sellers and one became the Amazon #1 New Release in Children's books. Prior to this book, his most recent release was *Life of a Stick Kid* - the fourth book in his children's book series.

His debut into writing was *Divorced Before 30* where he shares his story of overcoming the challenges of divorce, moving forward, and becoming a better version of himself.

His blog is focused on content that allows you to be 1% better each day whether you are a full-time entrepreneur or have a job with a side hustle. No fluff - just practical tools, tips, and principles that can be implemented today.

He started writing because of his two kids. They might even think he is cool now...maybe... probably not.

Join him at EdEscoto.com. You can also text him, 310.774.7992.

Made in the USA
Middletown, DE
24 September 2018